Bond
No.1 for exam success

SATs Skills

Grammar and Punctuation Workbook

9–10 years

OXFORD
UNIVERSITY PRESS

Great Clarendon Street, Oxford, OX26DP, United Kingdom

Oxford University Press is a department of the University of Oxford.
It furthers the University's objective of excellence in research, scholarship,
and education by publishing worldwide. Oxford is a registered trade mark
of Oxford University Press in the UK and in certain other countries

British Library Cataloguing in Publication Data
Data available

978-0-19-274560-6

10 9 8 7 6 5 4

Paper used in the production of this book is a natural, recyclable product
made from wood grown in sustainable forests. The manufacturing process
conforms to the environmental regulations of the country of origin.

Printed in China

Acknowledgements

Cover illustrations: Lo Cole

Although we have made every effort to trace and contact all copyright
holders before publication this has not been possible in all cases. If notified,
the publisher will rectify any errors or omissions at the earliest opportunity.

Links to third party websites are provided by Oxford in good faith and for
information only. Oxford disclaims any responsibility for the materials
contained in any third party website referenced in this work.

A) Add 'er' and 'est' to these adjectives to make comparative and superlative adjectives. [8]

Example: *fast*   *faster*   *fastest*

1 weak   _____   _____

2 clever   _____   _____

3 calm   _____   _____

4 hard   _____   _____

5 old   _____   _____

6 fair   _____   _____

7 poor   _____   _____

8 smart   _____   _____

> An **adjective** is a word that gives more information about a noun.
>
> **Comparative adjectives** are used to compare two things. We usually add 'er' to make the **comparative**.
>
> **Superlative adjectives** are used to compare more than two things. We often add 'est' to make the **superlative**.
>
> **Example:** Poppy is strong (**adjective**), Aaron is stronger (**comparative**) but Louise is strongest (**superlative**).

B) Put an apostrophe after the 's' to show plural possession. [10]

Example: *Those coats have got pockets.* *Those coats' pockets.*

1 Our cats have collars.   _____

2 These houses have red doors.   _____

3 Those trains have windows.   _____

4 The girls have books.   _____

5 The families have caravans.   _____

6 The zoos have animals.   _____

7 Those boats have sails.   _____

8 These cars have new tyres.   _____

9 The shops have customers.   _____

10 The printers have ink.   _____

> An apostrophe can be used to show when something belongs to someone. This is called '**possession**'.
>
> If the object has a single owner, the apostrophe is placed in front of the 's'.
>
> **Example:** Kasem's book.
>
> If the object has **plural** owners (more than one owner), the apostrophe goes after the 's'.
>
> **Example:** The boys have a holiday. The boys' holiday.

18

C Turn these simple past tense sentences into present perfect sentences by using 'has' or 'have' and the correct form of the verb given in capitals. [8]

Example: *(TEACH) She has taught that class.*

1   (SEE) We _____ that programme before.

2   (BUY) He _____ a new jacket for the winter.

3   (CATCH) They _____ a bus into the town centre.

4   (FILL) She _____ the bath with too much water.

5   (WRITE) I _____ an email to my best friend.

6   (GO) Mum _____ to the gym every Friday.

7   (FLY) My sister _____ to Australia for her holiday.

8   (FINISH) We _____ our project about volcanoes.

Verbs show whether something is happening now (the present) or in the past. Regular **verbs** in the **simple past tense** often end with 'ed' but irregular **verbs** change their spelling instead. For example, 'catch' becomes 'caught'. The **present perfect tense** is made from a main **verb** and a helper **verb** such as 'be', 'do' or 'have'. It shows that something has happened at some time in the past. It uses the **simple past tense** with either 'has' or 'have' before it.

Simple past tense	Present perfect
She visited the museum.	She has visited the museum.

D Underline the prepositions in these sentences. [6]

Example: *The bus drove <u>through</u> the village and <u>over</u> the bridge.*

1   *The dragon stomped around the woods, breathing fire on the ancient trees.*

2   *Jack and Harry tiptoed up the stairs and hid in the bedroom.*

3   *Kim lives across the road and down the hill.*

4   *Ali and Esther walked from the house to the shops.*

5   *Bella cycled with her parents to the playground.*

6   *Caleb sat beside his best friend, Seb, and behind his younger sister, Amy.*

A **preposition** often describes the position of a noun in a sentence.

Example: behind, on, under, beside, with, by, over. **Prepositions** help to give detail to our writing.

14

Underline the determiner in each sentence then write whether it is an article, demonstrative, number, ordinal, possessive adjective or quantifier. [10]

Example: *I don't need any money.* quantifier

1   I would like to order a taxi, please.   _____

2   I bought three birthday cards.   _____

3   We put away their clothes.   _____

4   Emily poured some juice.   _____

5   Have you got any biscuits?   _____

6   Shall I wear these shoes?   _____

7   Can you explain what happens next?   _____

8   I go swimming every Sunday.   _____

9   What have you done with your shoes?   _____

10   This soup is cold!   _____

> A **determiner** is a word that is put in front of a noun to make information about the noun clear. There are several types of **determiner**.
>
> **Possessive adjectives:** my, your, his, her, its, our, their
> **Articles:** a, an, the
> **Quantifiers:** any, every, few, more, much, some
> **Ordinals:** first, second, next, last
> **Demonstratives:** that, these, this, those
> **Numbers:** one, thirteen, ten thousand

Underline the fronted adverbials in these sentences. [8]

Example: *As soon as we were ready, we all climbed into the coach.*

1   Whenever I go into town, I walk through the park.

2   During break, I spoke to Mr Patak.

3   Slowly but surely, the last marathon runner crossed the finishing line.

4   While Dad drove to the campsite, I followed our route on the map.

5   As long as I concentrate, I should be able to knit myself a scarf.

6   Although I am not keen on coffee or tea, I do enjoy a nice mug of hot chocolate.

7   In spite of the cold, I enjoyed my walk at the nature reserve.

8   Unfortunately, the shed roof leaks when it rains.

> An **adverb** is a word that can add information to a **verb**. When a **phrase** (a group of words that does not include a **verb**) containing an **adverb** is put in front of the main part of the sentence, it can be called a **'fronted adverbial'**. A **fronted adverbial** is followed by a **comma**.
>
> **Example:** Before I go to bed, I always brush my teeth.

18

Ⓖ Write out these sentences using commas to separate the extra information from the main clause. [5]

Example: *Amy who enjoys hill walking climbed Bidston Hill to see the observatory.*

> Amy, who enjoys hill walking, climbed Bidston Hill to see the observatory.

1   Our old dog who has arthritis plodded up the road.

_____

2   The bungalow which was painted bright yellow looked cheerful.

_____

3   The new cafe just off the High Street sells delicious sandwiches.

_____

4   Northumberland with its amazing landscape is the perfect place to explore.

_____

5   The Welsh choir who come from Cardiff performed at the concert.

_____

Commas can separate items in a list and can help to make the meaning in a sentence clear. Like brackets, **commas** can also be used in pairs to give extra information that is not part of the **main clause**. A **main clause** is sometimes called an independent clause. (A **clause** contains a **verb** and gives the most important information in a sentence.)

Example:
My best friend (a rescue dog called Rex) loves to play ball in the park.
My best friend, a rescue dog called Rex, loves to play ball in the park.

Ⓗ Underline the main clauses in these compound sentences. [5]

Example: *Augustus was the first Roman Emperor and he ruled for 40 years.*

1   The Roman Empire was successful because its leaders were powerful.

2   The Romans invaded Europe, Africa and Asia and the Empire lasted for over 500 years.

3   Caligula was the third Roman emperor but he was assassinated at the age of 29.

4   Gordian ruled for only three weeks before he was killed in the Battle of Carthage.

5   The Romans left Britain over 1,600 years ago but their influence still remains in our language and laws.

A **main clause** can stand alone as a sentence. A **compound sentence** is made from two or more **clauses** joined with a **conjunction**. A **conjunction** is a joining word such as 'and', 'or', 'but', 'if' or 'yet'.

10

A Add 'er' and 'est' to these adjectives to make comparative and superlative adjectives. [8]

Example: slow   *slower*   *slowest*

1 long   _____   _____

2 quick   _____   _____

3 dull   _____   _____

4 sweet   _____   _____

5 rich   _____   _____

6 weird   _____   _____

7 harsh   _____   _____

8 sharp   _____   _____

B Turn these simple past tense sentences into present perfect sentences by using 'has' or 'have' and the correct form of the verb given in capitals. [8]

Example: (SEE) They *have seen* the pandas at the zoo.

1 (EAT) We _____ all the cheese and bread rolls.

2 (DRINK) He _____ a whole glass of milk!

3 (RUN) They _____ around the track really quickly.

4 (BUY) I _____ some new decorations for the Christmas tree.

5 (FIGHT) He _____ with almost everyone!

6 (FETCH) Mum _____ the shopping from the car.

7 (SEND) I _____ the parcel to my friend in Australia.

8 (FOLLOW) We _____ his progress on his online blog.

Helpful Hint

Remember to add the words 'has' or 'have' before the **verb** to make the **present perfect** form. The spelling of the **verb** can sometimes change if it is an irregular **verb**.

16

Ⓒ Place a colon in the correct places in the text below. [4]

Example: *You will need several ingredients flour, sugar, milk and butter.*

You will need several ingredients: flour, sugar, milk and butter.

1 My teacher has a saying "A colon is a very useful piece of punctuation."

2 ETHAN   You're going in the wrong direction!

3 There are three things you should bring a drink, some food, a sun hat.

4 Step 4 for baking a cake combine the wet and dry ingredients.

Using a **colon** (:) can help to improve the quality of writing. **Colons** can be used:

- before introducing bullet points (like these!)
- before an explanation
- before introducing a list after a **main clause**
- after the speaking character's name in a playscript
- before introducing a quotation.

Ⓓ Underline the prepositions in these sentences. [4]

Example: *Hayden ran <u>around</u> the field then <u>along</u> the track.*

1 The wind blew across the fields and through the trees.

2 We lived beyond the town, beside the river.

3 Freddie's kite flew above the treetops as he ran over the field.

4 The fish swam below the surface of the water and darted under the bridge.

Helpful Hint

Remember that a **preposition** explains the position of the noun.

Ⓔ Put commas in the correct places to make these sentences clear. [5]

Example: *"Do you want to eat Edward?"*

"Do you want to eat, Edward?"

A **comma** (,) is used to make sure the meaning in writing is clear.

1 Each morning I shower eat and get to school by nine.

2 Solomon loves drawing playing football and going to the cinema.

3 Knitting my family and my tortoise make me happy.

4 No skateboarding horses or quad bikes.

5 I bought some cabbage cake and coffee today.

13

Underline the main clauses in these compound sentences. [5]

Example: *Ava was given an award as she had worked really hard.*

1 Georges Hébert was a pioneer in PE as he developed the 'natural method'.

2 He was born in Paris in 1875 although he travelled extensively in his job.

3 He observed different tribes and he believed that nature was the best gym.

4 The natural method used movement but it focused on dangerous exercises.

5 Free-runners today run and jump off buildings yet they owe much to Hébert's method.

💡 **Helpful Hint**

Remember that a **compound sentence** has two or more **clauses** and a **conjunction**.

Ⓖ Write out these sentences, placing a semi-colon between the two clauses. [6]

Example: *The little boat bobbed up and down the fisherman prepared for a busy day.*

The little boat bobbed up and down; the fisherman prepared for a busy day.

1 Joe was very thirsty he had been cycling for hours.

_____

2 The door creaked open a strange figure appeared.

_____

3 Lexie laughed the dog was doing the strangest tricks!

_____

4 Elliott was really tired he had been ironing all afternoon.

_____

5 The allotment was productive we had so much to eat.

_____

6 I grow herbs in pots they are useful in cooking.

_____

A **semi-colon** (;) can link two or more related **clauses** instead of using a **conjunction**.

Example: Taylor left the window open; there was paper everywhere!

A **semi-colon** can also be used in a list that already contains **commas**.

Example: We invited Toby, a teacher; Kim, a carpenter; Father Pete, the local priest; and Tomak, a fisherman.

11

Ⓗ Change these third person sentences into the first person. [8]

Example: *He was so tired.* I was so tired.

1   Nur brought a newspaper with him.

_____

2   Rupert laughed so hard he couldn't breathe!

_____

3   They went to their local shops.

_____

4   She was out on her bike.

_____

5   He painted his picture.

_____

6   His shoes were muddy after his walk.

_____

7   Their car broke down at the end of their road.

_____

8   Ana lost her way in the dark.

_____

> Information or stories can be written from different points of view using the first, second or **third person**. The pronouns (words used to replace a noun) and **verbs** have to change to agree: when writing in the **first person,** the first-person pronouns have to be used so they agree with the first-person **verbs.**
>
> - In the **first person,** the pronouns used include 'I', 'me', 'my', 'we', 'us', 'our' and 'ours'.
>   **Example:** I recommend this games console.
> - In the **second person,** the pronouns used include 'you', 'your', and 'yours'.
>   **Example:** You will have to sign the form.
> - In the **third person,** the pronouns used include 'he', 'she', 'him', 'her', 'his', 'hers', 'it', 'its', 'their', 'theirs', 'them', 'they' or a name.
>   **Example:** Dan was feeling sad. It was the last day of his holiday.

Ⓘ Underline the phrase in each sentence. [6]

Example: *The curtains were drawn <u>across the tall, imposing windows</u>.*

1   Mr Crocket walked the dog through the coppice.

2   Mum made a special meal for Jacob's birthday.

3   We ate our soup from big, steaming bowls.

4   Along the pretty path of primroses, Lia lost her watch.

5   It was too dangerous to play football on the soggy, wet pitch.

6   I finally put my letter in the postbox.

> Words, **phrases** and **clauses** are used to build sentences. A **phrase** does not have a **verb** and it gives extra, descriptive information. A **clause** does have a **verb** and it gives the most important information.

14

A Double the last letter and then add 'er' and 'est' to these adjectives to make comparative and superlative adjectives. [5]

Example: *big*   *bigger*   *biggest*

1   thin   _____   _____

2   wet   _____   _____

3   red   _____   _____

4   fat   _____   _____

5   hot   _____   _____

> If an **adjective** ends in a single consonant and the letter before it is a single vowel with a short letter sound, double the last letter before adding 'er' or 'est' to make a **comparative** or **superlative adjective**.

B Write out these sentences using a comma after a subordinate clause. [5]

Example: *When you have brushed your teeth put your pyjamas on.*

When you have brushed your teeth, put your pyjamas on.

1   If you are not well go back to bed.

_____

2   Since you have finished your supper you can go out.

_____

3   Although we have planted that rose bush it won't flower until next summer.

_____

4   After the exams we will be going on a s chool residential trip.

_____

5   While you were at school I washed your PE kit.

_____

> A **subordinate clause** cannot stand alone as a sentence. It needs to go with a **main clause** to make sense. **Subordinate clauses** can be placed at the start, middle or end of a sentence and add extra information to the **main clause**. They are often separated from the **main clause** by a **comma**.

💡 **Helpful Hint**

Remember that **commas** have many uses: to make the meaning in writing clear; after most **subordinate clauses**; after a **fronted adverbial**; to separate items in a list.

10

C Write whether the underlined word is a common noun, proper noun, collective noun or abstract noun. [5]

Example: *We went to Whitby for a picnic.* proper noun

1 Shakespeare wrote many plays. _____

2 Our friendship began five years ago. _____

3 Lucas has a birthday in October. _____

4 The fleet of ships set sail. _____

5 Kieret grew strawberries on his allotment. _____

> A **common noun** is the general name of a person, place or thing.
>
> **Proper nouns** begin with a capital letter and include names of people, places, titles, days and months.
>
> A **collective noun** is a word for a group of nouns.
>
> An **abstract noun** refers to ideas or feelings.
>
> **Example:** dreams.

D Underline the determiner in each sentence, then write whether it is an article, demonstrative, number, ordinal, possessive adjective or quantifier. [4]

Example: *Have you got a card for Mo?* article

1 Have you seen her car? _____

2 The dog barked loudly. _____

3 I must paint this bench. _____

4 Would you like some soup? _____

E Place a colon in the correct place in these sentences. [3]

Example: *The ground is very dry it hasn't rained for a long time.*

    The ground is very dry: it hasn't rained for a long time.

1 You can use a range of ingredients in your curry turmeric, chilli, coriander and cumin.

2 Three areas are covered ancient history, medieval history, modern history.

3 He began to quote from Martin Luther King's speech "I have a dream …"

F Put an apostrophe after the 's' to show plural possession. [4]

Example: *Those pictures have frames.* Those pictures' frames.

1 My friends have games. _____

2 Those flowers have scent. _____

3 The tortoises have shells. _____

4 The knitters have wool. _____

16

3 Write out these sentences, placing a semi-colon between the two clauses. [3]

Example: The cyclist put on her helmet and reflective jacket the roads were busy.

The cyclist put on her helmet and reflective jacket; the roads were busy.

1 The guarantee was for a year the fridge broke down after thirteen months!

_____

2 The pony trotted to the trough he wanted a drink of water.

_____

3 Jamaica seems so far away thank goodness for the telephone.

_____

> **Helpful Hint**
>
> Remember that a **semi-colon** can link two or more related **clauses** instead of using a **conjunction.**

4 Underline the phrase in each sentence. [4]

Example: _Once upon a time,_ a woodcutter lived in that forest.

1 Last weekend we took our caravan to the Lake District.

2 Gordon was making everyone coffee, his usual task.

3 Although expensive, I bought the model kit.

4 In the end, Dad joined the cricket team.

> **Helpful Hint**
>
> Remember that a **phrase** is a group of words without a **verb.**

5 Turn these simple past tense sentences into present perfect sentences by using 'has' or 'have' and the correct form of the verb given in capitals. [4]

Example: *(SING) The boy has sung his solo.*

1 (MAKE) We _____ a curry for Dad's birthday.

2 (HEAR) He _____ the telephone ring.

3 (BRING) They _____ cakes into school for the cake sale.

4 (SLEEP) She _____ all night.

11

Quick quiz

1 Make a comparative and superlative adjective from the given adjective.

cold   _____   _____

2 Turn this simple past tense sentence into the present perfect using the correct form of the verb.

(WORK) We _____ hard on our presentation.

3 Use an apostrophe to show plural possession.

These girls have good manners. _____

4 Underline the best preposition for this sentence.

My little brother, George, played up/over/out/on/in the sandpit.

5 Underline the determiner in this sentence and then write what type of determiner it is.

I don't have much money left. _____

6 Underline the main clauses in this compound sentence.

The Hermitage Museum is in St Petersburg and it is an incredibly large building.

7 Underline the fronted adverbial in this sentence.

Although it is November, the leaves have not fallen off the trees.

8 Change the tense of this sentence from second to first person.

You saw the film at the cinema with your brother.

9 Underline the phrase in this sentence.

At the end of the evening, we had a wonderful meal.

10 Put a comma in the correct place in this sentence.

Although Yin was busy he always had time to help Kim with her project.

11 Put a semi-colon in the correct place in this sentence.

Micah had a little sister he really wanted a puppy.

12 Place a colon in the correct place in this sentence.

People have four main needs safety, shelter, food and companionship.

13–17 Add commas in the correct places in this paragraph.

Although Megan had struggled with the task she managed to create a beautifully scented perfume particularly for girls called 'Butterfly'. It was made with the essential oils of rose lily orange and lemon.

14

17

Ⓐ Turn these simple past tense sentences into present perfect sentences by using 'has' or 'have' and the correct form of the verb given in capitals. [8]

Example: *(FRIGHTEN) She has frightened herself silly!*

1 (VISIT) We _____ the Natural History Museum on a school trip.

2 (WALK) He _____ from Treorchy to Aberdare for charity.

3 (WEAR) They _____ animal costumes in the school play.

4 (SPEAK) She _____ to the girls' cricket team.

5 (BELONG) I _____ to the Brownies since I was seven.

6 (WIN) You _____ first prize in the raffle!

7 (RIDE) Joanna _____ her bicycle for three miles to reach my house.

8 (LOSE) Our school _____ the tennis tournament.

Ⓑ Underline the prepositions in these sentences. [8]

Example: *The hot air balloon floated up and into the distance.*

1 We ran along the road and then through the park.

2 Max searched for the monster among the flowers by the riverbank.

3 Josh and Nina crawled under the sheet and climbed into the den.

4 The girls hid behind the shed that stood in the orchard.

5 We climbed up the ladder and then slid down the slide.

6 We put the dirty clothes in the washing machine and turned it on.

7 I was after Ava in the queue.

8 He pushed the letter through the postbox then walked back down the path.

💡 **Helpful Hint**
Remember that a **preposition** describes where a noun is.

16

ⓒ Put an apostrophe after the 's' to show plural possession. [6]

Example: *The schools have teachers.* The schools' teachers.

1 The doors have keys. _____

2 These horses have saddles. _____

3 Those birds have nests. _____

4 The laptops have cases. _____

5 The bicycles have pedals. _____

6 These skirts have belts. _____

ⓓ Write out these sentences, placing a semi-colon between the two clauses. [6]

Example: *The window was open the bird flew in.*

The window was open; the bird flew in.

1 It was hot they decided to have a barbecue.

_____

2 The judge walked into the courtroom everyone stood up.

_____

3 Selina was feeling sad her son had caught a cold.

_____

4 The clock showed midnight he had still not returned from work.

_____

5 The washing machine was on they had spent a week camping in the rain.

_____

6 She filled the kettle she needed a cup of coffee.

_____

12

(E) Put commas in the correct places in these sentences. [5]

Example: *Luckily I remembered to take my keys with me.*

Luckily, I remembered to take my keys with me.

> **Commas** can be used to separate items in a list and at each end of a word or **phrase** that has been added to a sentence to give new and extra information. **Commas** can also be used after a short response at the beginning of a sentence.
>
> **Example:** Yes, I've added the sugar to the mix.

1   Before you go please put away your whiteboards.

2   Fortunately I had enough money for the bus fare home.

3   Yes I am going to go to the supermarket after work.

4   Violins cellos and double basses are all in the string section of an orchestra.

5   No I'm not sure when the train is due.

(F) Underline the fronted adverbials in these sentences. [5]

Example: *Once the team was ready, they walked onto the pitch.*

1   Thinking about Dad, I decided to buy pyjamas for his birthday.

2   Sitting on the train, I checked my emails.

3   Downloading another app, I wondered if it would help me with my homework.

4   Wheezing and sneezing, I climbed back into bed feeling very poorly.

5   Sitting down, Dodi took out her embroidery and began sewing.

> **Helpful Hint**
> Remember that a **fronted adverbial** is a **phrase** that begins a sentence and describes the action that comes after it.

(G) Underline the verbs and circle the adverbs in these sentences. [5]

Example: *James was (noisily) slurping his tea.*

1   Olivia toddled unsteadily across the floor.

2   Padraig nervously watched the crucial tennis match.

3   Sophia was sprawling lazily on the sofa.

4   Ishmael coldly explained that he was unhappy with his sister.

5   Melody leapt enthusiastically into the turquoise sea.

> **Helpful Hint**
> Remember, an **adverb** describes a **verb** and often ends with the letters 'ly'.

15

H Change the tense of these sentences from third to second person. [5]

Example: *She loves cake.* You love cake.

1 They have worked hard on their new extension.

_____

2 He went climbing with his friends on Saturday.

_____

3 Chrissy put on her swimming costume.

_____

4 Omar is playing in his bedroom.

_____

5 What did she do to deserve that?

_____

> ## Helpful Hint
>
> Remember to check whether you need to change the pronouns and **verbs** when you change from writing in the **third person** to the **second person**.

I Write the correct form of the verb in capitals to complete these sentences. [7]

Example: *(MAKE) Yesterday, I* made *a den in the garden.*

1 (SLEEP) I was so tired that I _____ until my alarm clock rang.

2 (KNEEL) I _____ down to pick up a pen and couldn't stand up again!

3 (RUN) Last week, we _____ around the park three times.

4 (DRINK) I was thirsty so I _____ a whole bottle of water.

5 (EAT) We were running late so we _____ supper when we got back.

6 (FIND) We _____ the puzzle really difficult!

7 (SELL) The shop _____ everything from stamps to picture frames.

It is important to make sure that the correct form of the **verb** is used in writing: you must use the correct tense.

Example: 'I am standing up' uses the **present tense,** but this would change to 'I stood up' in the **past tense**. The words 'stand', 'standing' and 'stood' are all forms of the same **verb** so it is important to choose the correct one.

12

Ⓐ Put an apostrophe after the 's' to show plural possession. [8]

Example: *The ponies have tails.* The ponies' tails.

1 Our villages have parks. _____

2 These shoes have laces. _____

3 Those gardens have flowers. _____

4 The bees have a hive. _____

5 The towns have roundabouts. _____

6 The cyclists have helmets. _____

7 The computers have software. _____

8 The rivers have bridges. _____

Ⓑ Underline the determiner in each sentence, then write whether it is an article, demonstrative, number, ordinal, possessive adjective or quantifier. [10]

Example: *We were last to leave.* ordinal

1 I have asked for more cake. _____

2 There are five poems to learn. _____

3 I am third in line for assembly. _____

4 There were twenty chickens for sale. _____

5 Is anybody sitting on this chair? _____

6 We have an apple crumble for pudding. _____

7 There are raisins in these cookies. _____

8 Have you seen my umbrella? _____

9 Is there a spare ticket? _____

10 Our cousins live in Bangladesh. _____

> 💡 **Helpful Hint**
>
> Remember that **determiners** are placed in front of the noun to help to make information about the noun clear.

18

C Put commas in the correct places in these sentences with direct speech. [8]

Example: *Uncle Rory said "I am watching the rugby match this afternoon."*

Uncle Rory said, "I am watching the rugby match this afternoon."

1 The announcer's voice boomed out "Here are your judges!"

2 "I've got cod, haddock, coley or pollock" said the fishmonger.

3 Dad shouted "Your supper's ready!"

4 Flynn and Sebastian both asked "Where is the cat?"

5 "Have a cup of tea" said Mrs Hastings softly.

6 Cameron asked "What time is your appointment?"

7 "But I don't understand" moaned Maisie.

8 "Be polite" their mother warned.

> **Commas** can be used in a **narrative** (a story) to separate what someone is saying (speech) from the rest of the sentence. **Inverted commas** are put around the words that a character says.
>
> Place a **comma** before the **closing inverted commas** when you **close** the **direct speech**.
>
> "Please come here⊙" said Mr Patel.
>
> Place a **comma** before the **opening inverted commas** when you **open** the **direct speech**.
>
> Alyssa called out⊙ "I'm just coming!"

D Place colons in the correct places in these questions. [6]

Example: *I sell several types of honey lavender, heather and wildflower honey.*

I sell several types of honey: lavender, heather and wildflower honey.

1–3 Act 2, Scene 3

Abdu	How did you get such a brilliant job?
Fareem	There were several reasons I studied hard, did my homework and revised for my exams.

4 The town centre has a wide range of shops a bakery, a bookshop, a chemist and an art gallery.

5 The day's activities will include
   • climbing
   • canoeing
   • swimming.

6 I have several favourite authors Michael Morpurgo, Eva Ibbotson, Chris Riddell and Jacqueline Wilson.

14

E) Underline the verbs and circle the adverbs in these sentences. [8]

Example: *Ruth stamped her feet crossly.*

1   Rob happily ran the shop in the village.

2   The old man climbed cautiously on the bus.

3   Zakeem sat patiently with his fishing rod.

4   Uncle Mo lovingly built a beautiful treehouse in the garden.

5   The ballerina gracefully leapt across the stage in her white tutu.

6   The timid, grey mouse scuttled nervously behind the cupboard.

7   The gentle breeze gradually dried the clothes on the washing line.

8   Hurriedly, the pedestrian crossed the busy road.

F) Write whether each underlined phrase is a noun phrase, a preposition phrase or a clause. [6]

Example: *On the road, we saw four sheep.* preposition phrase

1   In the hall of the mountain king, the trolls were eating a feast.

_____

2   The kitten, a pretty little thing, was clinging to the curtain.

_____

3   The babbling brook flowed under the old stone bridge.

_____

4   The couple danced a wonderful salsa.

_____

5   Flicking and swishing his long tail, the pony trotted up to the fence.

_____

6   We all went out for a lovely meal at the restaurant.

_____

A **phrase** is a group of words that gives additional information but does not include a **verb**.

A **noun phrase** gives more information about a noun.

A **clause** has a **verb** and give information.

A **preposition phrase** gives more information using a **preposition**.

A **phrase** with a **verb** at its head is called a **clause**.

14

Ⓖ Turn the positive sentences into negative sentences by adding or replacing words with 'never', 'nobody', 'not' or 'nothing'. [6]

Example: *We sometimes play cricket in the summer.*

We never play cricket in the summer.

A positive sentence gives information about what something is, has or does. A negative sentence also gives information but it uses words such as 'never', 'nobody', 'none', 'not' and 'nothing'.

1 My sister does have a driving lesson at the weekend.

_____

2 I saw something that interested me at the gallery.

_____

3 There was somebody in the park yesterday evening.

_____

4 There was some food left over after lunch.

_____

5 Ben always brushes his hair before he goes out.

_____

6 Dolores does like olives or anchovies.

_____

Ⓗ Underline the correct form of the verb to complete these sentences. [8]

Example: *We (enjoys/enjoying/enjoy) being in the music club.*

1 Camilla and Jimena (saw/see/seen) a majestic eagle.

2 We (was/were/am) surprised to hear he was moving to Canada.

3 I have been (give/given/giving) a new skateboard.

4 Rodrigo is (travel/travelled/travelling) to Spain for the summer holidays.

5 Have you (do/does/done) your homework today?

6 Our friend was (disappoint/disappointment/disappointed) when his favourite team was knocked out of the tournament.

7 Mrs Mencher (am/is/are) teaching us to speak Polish.

8 Alex (turn/turning/turned) off the lights before she left the house.

14

Answers

Unit 1

(A) 1 weaker, weakest
2 cleverer, cleverest
3 calmer, calmest
4 harder, hardest
5 older, oldest
6 fairer, fairest
7 poorer, poorest
8 smarter, smartest

(B) 1 Our cats' collars.
2 These houses' red doors.
3 Those trains' windows.
4 The girls' books.
5 The families' caravans.
6 The zoos' animals.
7 Those boats' sails.
8 These cars' new tyres.
9 The shops' customers.
10 The printers' ink.

(C) 1–8 have seen, has bought, have caught, has filled, have written, has gone, has flown, have finished

(D) 1 around, on
2 up, in
3 across, down
4 from, to
5 with, to
6 beside, behind

(E) 1 a, article
2 three, number
3 their, possessive adjective
4 some, quantifier
5 any, quantifier
6 these, demonstrative
7 next, ordinal
8 every, quantifier
9 your, possessive adjective
10 This, demonstrative

(F) 1 Whenever I go into town
2 During break
3 Slowly but surely
4 While Dad drove to the campsite
5 As long as I concentrate
6 Although I am not keen on coffee or tea
7 In spite of the cold
8 Unfortunately

(G) 1 ,who has arthritis,
2 ,which was painted in brighten yellow,
3 ,just off High Street,
4 ,with its amazing landscape,
5 ,who come from Cardiff,

(H) 1 The Roman Empire was successful, its leaders were powerful.
2 The Romans invaded Europe, Africa and Asia, the Empire lasted for over 500 years.
3 Caligula was the third Roman emperor, he was assassinated at the age of 29.
4 Gordian ruled for only three weeks, he was killed in the Battle of Carthage.
5 The Romans left Britain over 1600 years ago, their influence still remains in our language and laws.

Unit 2

(A) 1 longer, longest
2 quicker, quickest
3 duller, dullest
4 sweeter, sweetest
5 icher, richest
6 weirder, weirdest
7 harsher, harshest
8 sharper, sharpest

(B) 1 have eaten
2 has drunk
3 have run
4 have bought
5 has fought
6 has fetched
7 have sent
8 have followed

(C) 1 My teacher has a saying: "A colon is a very useful piece of punctuation".
2 ETHAN: You're going in the wrong direction!
3 There are three things you should bring: a drink, some food, a sun hat.
4 Step 4: combine the wet and dry ingredients.

(D) 1 across, through
2 beyond, beside
3 above, over
4 below, under

(E) 1 Each morning I shower, eat and get to school by nine.
2 Solomon loves drawing, playing football and going to the cinema.
3 Knitting, my family and my tortoise make me happy.
4 No skateboarding, horses or quad bikes.
5 I bought some cabbage, cake and coffee today.

(F) 1 Georges Hébert was a pioneer in PE, he developed the 'natural method'.
2 He was born in Paris in 1875, he travelled extensively in his job.
3 He observed different tribes, he believed that nature was the best gym.
4 The natural method used movement, it focused on dangerous exercises.
5 Free-runners today run and jump off buildings, they owe much to Hébert's method.

(G) 1 Joe was very thirsty; he had been cycling for hours.
2 The door creaked open; a strange figure appeared.
3 Lexie laughed; the dog was doing the strangest tricks!
4 Elliott was really tired; he had been ironing all afternoon.
5 The allotment was productive; we had so much to eat.
6 I grow herbs in pots; they are useful in cooking.

(H) 1 I brought a newspaper with me.
2 I laughed so hard I couldn't breathe!
3 We went to our local shops.
4 I was out on my bike.
5 I painted my picture.
6 My shoes were muddy after my walk.
7 Our car broke down at the end of our road.
8 I lost my way in the dark.

(I) 1 through the coppice
2 for Jacob's birthday
3 from big, steaming bowls
4 Along the pretty path of primroses
5 on the soggy, wet pitch
6 in the postbox

Unit 3

(A) 1 thinner, thinnest 2 wetter, wettest 3 redder, reddest 4 fatter, fattest 5 hotter, hottest

(B) 1 If you are not well, go back to bed.
2 Since you have finished your supper, you can go out.
3 Although we have planted that rose bush, it won't flower until next summer.
4 After the exams, we will be going on a school residential trip.
5 While you were at school, I washed your PE kit.

(C) 1 proper noun
2 abstract noun
3 proper noun
4 collective noun
5 common noun

(D) 1 her, possessive adjective
2 The, article
3 this, demonstrative
4 some, quantifier

(E) 1 You can use a range of ingredients in your curry: turmeric, chilli, coriander and cumin.
2 Three areas are covered: ancient history, medieval history, modern history.
3 He began to quote from Martin Luther King's speech: "I have a dream …"

(F) 1 My friends' games.
2 Those flowers' scent.
3 The tortoises' shells.
4 The knitters' wool

(G) 1 The guarantee was for a year; the fridge broke down after thirteen months!

2 The pony trotted to the trough; he wanted a drink of water.

3 Jamaica seems so far away; thank goodness for the telephone.

(H) 1 Last weekend   3 Although expensive

2 his usual task   4 In the end

(I) 1 have made   2 has heard   3 have brought   4 has slept

Quick quiz

1 colder, coldest   2 have worked

3 These girls' good manners.   4 in   5 much, quantifier

6 The Hermitage Museum is in St Petersburg and it is an incredibly large building.

7 Although it is November

8 I saw the film at the cinema with my brother.

9 At the end of the evening

10 Although Yin was busy, he always had time to help Kim with her project.

11 Micah had a little sister; he really wanted a puppy.

12 People have four main needs: safety, shelter, food and companionship.

13–17 Although Megan had struggled with the task, she managed to create a beautifully scented perfume, particularly for girls, called 'Butterfly'. It was made with the essential oils of rose, lily, orange and lemon.

Unit 4

(A) 1 have visited   2 has walked   3 have worn
4 has spoken   5 have belonged   6 have won   7 has ridden
8 has lost

(B) 1 along, through   4 behind, in   7 after, in
2 among, by   5 up, down   8 through, down
3 under, into   6 in, on

(C) 1 The doors' keys.   4 The laptops' cases.
2 These horses' saddles.   5 The bicycles' pedals.
3 Those birds' nests.   6 These skirts' belts.

(D) 1 It was hot; they decided to have a barbecue.

2 The judge walked into the courtroom; everyone stood up.

3 Selina was feeling sad; her son had caught a cold.

4 The clock showed midnight; he had still not returned from work.

5 The washing machine was on; they had spent a week camping in the rain.

6 She filled the kettle; she needed a cup of coffee.

(E) 1 Before you go, please put away your whiteboards.

2 Fortunately, I had enough money for the bus fare home.

3 Yes, I am going to go to the supermarket after work.

4 Violins, cellos and double basses are all in the string section of an orchestra.

5 No, I'm not sure when the train is due.

(F) 1 Thinking about Dad   4 Wheezing and sneezing
2 Sitting on the train   5 Sitting down
3 Downloading another app

(G) 1–5 toddled, unsteadily; nervously watched; sprawling, lazily; coldly, explained; leapt, enthusiastically

(H) 1 You have worked hard on your new extension.

2 You went climbing with your friends on Saturday.

3 You put on your swimming costume.

4 You are playing in your bedroom.

5 What did you do to deserve that?

(I) 1–7 slept, knelt, ran, drank, ate, found, sold

Unit 5

(A) 1 Our villages' parks.   2 These shoes' laces.
3 Those gardens' flowers.   4 The bees' hive.   5 The towns' roundabouts.   6 The cyclists' helmets.   7 The computers' software.   8 The rivers' bridges

(B) 1 more, quantifier   6 an, article
2 five, number   7 these, demonstrative
3 third, ordinal   8 my, possessive adjective
4 twenty, number   9 a, article
5 this, demonstrative   10 Our, possessive adjective

(C) 1 The announcer's voice boomed out, "Here are your judges!"

2 "I've got cod, haddock, coley or pollock," said the fishmonger.

3 Dad shouted, "Your supper's ready!"

4 Flynn and Sebastian both asked, "Where is the cat?"

5 "Have a cup of tea," said Mrs Hastings softly.

6 Cameron asked, "What time is your appointment?"

7 "But I don't understand," moaned Maisie.

8 "Be polite," their mother warned.

(D) 1–3 Act 2, Scene 3

Abdu: How did you get such a brilliant job?

Fareem: There were several reasons: I studied hard, did my homework and revised for my exams.

4 The town centre has a wide range of shops: a bakery, a bookshop, a chemist and an art gallery.

5 The day's activities will include:

• climbing

• canoeing

• swimming.

6 I have several favourite authors: Michael Morpurgo, Eva Ibbotson, Chris Riddell and Jacqueline Wilson.

(E) 1 happily ran; climbed cautiously; sat patiently; lovingly built; gracefully leapt; scuttled nervously; gradually dried; Hurriedly crossed

(F) 1-3 preposition phrase, noun phrase, preposition phrase
4-6 clause, clause, preposition phrase

(G) 1 My sister does not have a driving lesson at the weekend.

2 I saw nothing / did not see anything that interested me at the gallery.

3 There was nobody / wasn't anybody in the park yesterday evening.

4 There was no / wasn't any food left over after lunch.

5 Ben never brushes his hair before he goes out.

6 Dolores does not like olives or anchovies.

(H) 1 saw   2 were   3 given   4 travelling   5 done
6 disappointed   7 is   8 turned

Unit 6

(A) 1-4 noun phrase, clause, clause, preposition phrase

(B) 1 later, latest   2 stranger, strangest   3 wiser, wisest
4 bluer, bluest

A2

C 1 Our countries' borders. 2 This hotel's garden.
3 These phones' cases.

D 1 The recipe needs flour, self-raising; eggs, medium or large; sugar, caster is best but any will do; butter, salted or unsalted.

2 You will need a pot, one with large drainage holes; soil, add feed; some plants, bright colours are best.

3 We played 'Pass the parcel', which Anya won; 'Musical chairs', which Archie won; 'Musical statues', which Lauren won.

E 1 The weather was pleasant.

2 He looked like his cousin Denny.

3 We have seen that programme before.

4 I do want to go to the party.

F 1–4 are, was, saw, said

G 1–4 frantically, sped; politely, ate; dramatically, narrated; twinkle, magically

H 1–4 Before you go to bed, After lunch, whenever I am in town, During the night

I 1 shinier, shiniest   3 tinier, tiniest   5 lumpier, lumpiest
2 easier, easiest   4 funnier, funniest

Quick quiz

1 The horses' stables. 2 My team's coach.
3 The Christmas tree's lights. 4 no 5 not 6 not 7 never
8 has 9 play 10 did 11 clause 12 preposition phrase
13 clause 14 Mr Smith said, "I would like to leave now."
15 Unless they have permission, pupils may not leave the school at lunchtime. 16 Although we were late, the doctor still saw us.

Unit 7

A 1–10 were thinking, was singing, were jumping, was viewing, was catching, were cantering, was rehearsing, was lighting, were chasing, was racing

B 1 A noun is thing, place or person.

2 A verb is an action word; a doing word.

3 An adverb gives more information about a verb.

4 An adjective gives more information about a noun.

5 A preposition tells us the position of a noun.

6 A pronoun is a word that replaces a noun.

7 A conjunction joins clauses together.

C 1 We visited the beach, even though it was windy, as it was sheltered.

2 Apart from Sunday, I don't think it rained at all last week.

3 This shop has branches in Bath, Bristol, Cardiff and Penzance.

4 Rudolph said, "Why am I the only reindeer with a red nose?"

D 1 clause 2 noun phrase 3 preposition phrase
4 preposition phrase

E 1 We buy cupcakes and macaroons from the bakery.

2 Whenever I visit Loren we spend the time talking.

3 The two blocks of flats stand on the outskirts of town.

4 We must see our cousins this summer.

5 We like to paddle in the sea when we go on holiday.

F 1 among, in   3 near, before   5 near, underneath
2 on, down   4 up, beside

G 1 the, article   6 her, possessive adjective
2 my, possessive adjective   7 a, article
3 any, quantifier   8 some, quantifier
4 eight, number   9 fourth, ordinal
5 the, article   10 this, demonstrative

H 1–8 was, eat, perform, saw, finished, heard, rose, am

Unit 8

A 1 The navy has different types of ship: destroyers, frigates, survey ships and mine hunters.

2 Of all the museums, the submarine museum is our favourite.

3 You can do a guided tour, explore as a group or wander at leisure.

4 If you are not scared of small spaces, go on board the 1901 midget submarine.

5 "Well," said Jay, "shall we go and have a look?"

B 1–6 were sleeping, was reading, were sketching, was teaching, was gnawing, were catching

C 1 grumbled, constantly; ate, greedily; tumbled, awkwardly; Impressively, won; studiously, completed; Fortunately, remembered

D 1 Before we went to bed, we brushed our teeth.

2 After the thunder, the lightning lit up the dark sky.

3 Along the cycle path, Nina rode her bike.

4 All morning, we waited for the post to arrive.

5 Before I could catch it, the plate smashed on the floor.

6 When it was empty, Kai refilled the bird feeder.

7 Cleaning her room, Ana found her reading book.

E 1 The rain fell continually, it certainly seemed that way.

2 Grey clouds had been gathering for days, we knew the rain was coming.

3 Abi was really tired, it had been a long day.

4 She'd had a great time with her friends, she hadn't seen them for ages.

5 Sammy hoped she could complete the marathon, she had trained so hard.

6 She had never taken on such a big challenge, her mum was sure she could do it.

7 There was a long queue at the post office, I went back later.

8 My auntie lives in India, she is coming to stay with us for a holiday.

F 1 It is important in a busy urban area to have green spaces: they are a place for children to play and for people to meet each other.

2 If you are responsible for a park, it is important to:
• make sure that plants are pruned so walkways are safe
• provide bins for litter and dog waste
• provide staff to monitor the park for signs of danger.

3 There are several poisonous plants: hemlock, yew, foxgloves and laurel.

4 He recited from Wordsworth's famous poem: "I wandered lonely as a cloud …"

5 You will need to bring two of the following forms of identification: driving licence, passport, bank statement.

G 1–12 *Each adjective should be preceded by 'more' and 'most', e.g.* more important (comparative) *and* most important (superlative).

(H) 1 Mrs Rand's toast and Mr Rand's cereal.

2 Those shops' bargains and this shop's best prices.

3 Our family's tents and those families' caravans.

4 Tinkerbell's magic wand and Peter's tuneful pipe.

5 The cats' new toys and the dog's new bed.

6 The villages' playing fields and the town's swimming pool.

7 The planes' wings and the helicopters' rotor blades.

8 The phone's camera and the computer's printer.

9 The book's chapters and the chapters' paragraphs.

10 The artist's brushes and the writers' pens.

Unit 9

(A) 1 A person who studies flies, as opposed to all insects, is a dipterist.

2 No, I did not know that the French word for fly is 'mouche'.

3 The teacher said, "There are more than 7000 types of fly in the UK."

4 Although they only live for a month, a housefly goes through four life stages.

5 Many different flies are found in the UK: lacewings, bluebottles, horseflies and houseflies.

(B) 1–6 were running, was knitting, was hoping, were talking, were ripping, was going

(C) 1 the, article 4 my, possessive adjective

2 my, possessive adjective 5 any, quantifier

3 much, quantifier 6 every, quantifier

(D) 1 (happily), playing; spoke,(earnestly); strode, (steadily); (successfully), taught; fluttered,(gently),(skilfully), painted

(E) 1 It is the big football match today, the town centre will be busy.

2 We had our hair cut, our usual hairdresser was not there.

3 You could have some fruit, you may prefer to have yoghurt instead.

4 I have never been to Canada, I would love to go there.

5 The Highlands of Scotland are amazing, they can be dangerous in the winter months.

6 I am going to Charlotte's party, my cousin is also invited.

(F) 1 We had a collection of buckets and spades; we took building sandcastles seriously.

2 Jessie had a new football game; she couldn't wait to try it.

3 The boys were very noisy; they were disturbing everyone.

4 Tavleen was excited; she had new shoes to wear for the celebrations.

5 Jasper loved painting; he mixed blue and red to make deep purple.

(G) 1 Phoebe visited her aunt in Norwich.

2 Stacey did have time to rest before the next race.

3 Logan saw his friends at the swimming pool.

4 Kit and Seb did get on the train.

(H) 1 The ring was irresistible for the thief so he stole it.

2 Footballers have a fitness regime so they are able to perform at their best.

3 We went hover-boarding on holiday!

4 Scientists are researching how to repair nerves, which will help people with pain or nerve damage.

5 Paul walked across the hills and saw wildlife in Yorkshire.

6 I felt nervous in front of an audience.

7 The firelight flickered in the darkness.

8 Music was playing on the radio.

Unit 10

1 sunnier, sunniest 2 more adaptable, most adaptable

3 braver, bravest 4 bought 5 knew 6 poured

7 in, by 8 near, beside 9 first, ordinal 10 a, article

11 that, demonstrative 12 five, number

13 Daffodils are spring bulbs, dahlias are summer bulbs.

14 Mixing blue and yellow makes green, varying the amount of each colour changes the shade.

15 Hockey is played with a stick, tennis is played with a racquet.

16 Although the scenery was fantastic

17 Whenever we go camping 18 However

19 As long as you are home by teatime

20 Haru and Tom visited Alex; he had been ill with the flu.

21 The wood panelling was gorgeous; it was typical of a Tudor building.

22 I was off to my gymnastics class.

23 We were playing with Alima in her garden.

24 I stubbed my toe against the table leg.

25–28 (steadily) swam,(generously) shared; packed, (solidly); smiled,(broadly)

29 baked 30 went 31 broke 32 Noun phrase

33 Preposition phrase

34 My bedroom is never neat and tidy.

35 There is nothing you can do to get ready for the holiday.

36 This book's torn cover. 37 Those jars' labels.

38 These elephants' trunks.

39 The brook flowed into the river.

40 The sound of Rupa's alarm clock woke her.

41 The hand-knitted blanket was in shades of pink, cream, purple and blue.

42 Rosie said, "Yes, I enjoy crafts but it is hard to find time for them all!"

43 The little babies, all lying in their cots, slept contentedly.

44 "I know," said Mrs David sympathetically."It can be really tricky," she continued.

45 Miss Dembenski's poster has a great message: "Always do your best and that is enough."

46 There are four things you need: a pencil, ruler, pen and eraser.

47 Sherry is a lovely horse: she has such a gentle manner.

48 You should:

- write your name on each page
- read each question carefully
- answer every question
- check your answers before you hand in your paper.

49 Marly's book. 50 The flock's shepherd.

51 Our bicycles' wheels.

(A) Write whether the underlined words are noun phrase, a preposition phrase or a clause. [4]

Example: _Barney and Grandpa walked briskly past the village hall._ *clause*

1   The cathedral, <u>with its Gothic steeple</u>, has beautiful stained glass.

_____

2   <u>Visitors can climb to the top</u>, if they have enough energy.

_____

3   <u>I climbed the steps carefully</u> because it had been raining. until I reached the roof.

_____

4   The squirrel ran <u>along the rooftops</u>.

_____

> 💡 **Helpful Hint**
>
> Remember, a **noun phrase** describes the noun and a **preposition phrase** gives additional information using a **preposition**. A **phrase** with a **verb** as its head is a **clause**.

(B) Add 'er' and 'est' to these adjectives to make the comparative and superlative adjectives. [4]

Example: *close*   *closer*   *closest*

1 late	_____	_____
2 strange	_____	_____
3 wise	_____	_____
4 blue	_____	_____

> ℹ️ To create **comparative** and **superlative adjectives** for words that already end in 'e', first drop the 'e' then add 'er' or 'est'.

(C) Write out these sentences adding an apostrophe in the right place to show single or plural possession. [3]

Example: _The soldiers have boots._ The soldiers' boots.

1   Our countries have borders.   _____

2   This hotel has a garden.   _____

3   These phones have cases.   _____

11

D Write out these sentences using commas and semi-colons to divide the items in each list. [3]

> **Commas** can separate items in a list. **Semi-colons** can separate items in a list that already use **commas**. They mark the boundary between the items.
>
> **Example:** The group includes Paige, a flautist; Olly, a clarinettist; Rueben, a bassoonist.

Example: *We travelled to Tangier in Morocco Cadiz in Spain and Nice in France.*

We travelled to Tangier, in Morocco; Cadiz, in Spain; and Nice, in France.

1   The recipe needs flour self-raising eggs medium or large sugar caster is best but any will do butter salted or unsalted.

_____

_____

_____

2   You will need a pot one with large drainage holes soil add feed some plants bright colours are best.

_____

_____

_____

3   We played 'Pass the parcel' which Anya won 'Musical chairs' which Archie won 'Musical statues' which Lauren won.

_____

_____

_____

E Turn the negative sentences into positive sentences by removing the words 'never', 'none', 'not' or 'nothing'. [4]

> To turn a negative sentence into a positive sentence, replace or remove negative words such as 'never', 'nobody', 'none', 'not' and 'nothing'.

Example: *I never go into town on Saturdays.*

I go into town on Saturdays.

1   The weather was not pleasant.

_____

2   He looked nothing like his cousin Denny.

_____

3   We have never seen that programme before.

_____

4   I do not want to go to the party.

_____

7

F Underline the correct form of the verb to complete these sentences. [4]

Example: I <u>am</u>/are going to win the competition!

1 We am/are going to the cinema tonight!

2 I was/were going to call you later.

3 Estefan saw/seen his cousin last week.

4 She said/say I had to go to the back of the queue.

G Underline the verbs and circle the adverbs in these sentences. [4]

Example: The boy <u>crept</u> (softly) behind the statue.

1 The red lorry frantically sped down the hill.

2 The quiet child politely ate his banana sandwiches.

3 Mrs Anderson dramatically narrated the latest adventure.

4 Our solar lights twinkle magically among the honeysuckle and ivy.

H Underline the fronted adverbials in these sentences. [4]

Example: <u>When you have finished</u>, remember to tidy up.

1 Before you go to bed, get everything ready for tomorrow.

2 After lunch, you can use the computer.

3 Whenever I am in town, I always visit the library.

4 During the night, the foxes played in the garden.

I Replace the 'y' with 'i' before adding 'er' and 'est' to make comparative and superlative adjectives. [5]

Example: heavy   *heavier*   *heaviest*

1 shiny   _____   _____

2 easy   _____   _____

3 tiny   _____   _____

4 funny   _____   _____

5 lumpy   _____   _____

> If an adjective ends in a 'y', remove the 'y' and replace it with an 'i' before adding 'er' or 'est' to make **comparative** and **superlative adjectives**.

17

Quick quiz

Put an apostrophe in the right place to show single or plural possession.

1 The horses have stables. _____

2 My team has a coach. _____

3 The Christmas tree has lights. _____

Turn these positive sentences into negative sentences by adding one negative word in the space.

4 Khalid has _____ cake with his coffee.

5 Sam does _____ enjoy reading.

6 Carla did _____ eat all day.

7 I _____ look good in photographs!

Underline the correct form of the verb to complete these sentences.

8 Jem has/have no credit on his phone.

9 We play/plays the piano every day.

10 They did/done their maths exam.

Write whether the underlined words are a noun phrase, a preposition phrase or a clause.

11 If I'm not too tired, <u>I will make dinner tonight</u>.

_____

12 <u>Underneath the apple tree</u>, the boys sat quietly and read.

_____

13 Despite the sad ending, <u>Clare really enjoyed the play</u>.

_____

Put commas in the correct place in these sentences.

14 Mr Smith said "I would like to leave now."

15 Unless they have permission pupils may not leave the school at lunchtime.

16 Although we were late the doctor still saw us.

16

A) Fill in the gaps in the sentences using the past progressive form of the verb given in capitals. [10]

Example: *(STICK) I was sticking a poster on the wall.*

1 (THINK) They _____ about their holidays.

2 (SING) Joanna _____ in the shower.

3 (JUMP) The girls _____ over the hurdles.

4 (VIEW) Oscar _____ the new house.

5 (CATCH) Dominik _____ a cold from his sister.

6 (CANTER) The horses _____ around the field.

7 (REHEARSE) Liu _____ her part in the school play.

8 (LIGHT) Natalia _____ the candles on the cake.

9 (CHASE) The dogs _____ one another in the park.

10 (RACE) Mum _____ round the supermarket before it closed.

> The progressive form of a **verb** describes an event that is in progress.
>
> **Example:** I am swimming.
>
> If the action happened in the past, the **verb** needs to be changed to the past tense, using 'was' or 'were' and the 'ing' ending of the **verb**.
>
> **Example:** I was swimming.

B) Use a line to join each word with its definition. [7]

1 A noun   joins clauses together.

2 A verb   gives more information about a verb.

3 An adverb   is a word that replaces a noun.

4 An adjective   is a thing, place or person.

5 A preposition   gives more information about a noun.

6 A pronoun   is an action word; a doing word.

7 A conjunction   tells us the position of a noun.

17

(c) Write out these sentences, adding commas in the correct places. [4]

Example: *Built in the 1950s our house is the oldest in the street.*

Built in the 1950s, our house is the oldest in the street.

1 We visited the beach even though it was windy as it was sheltered.

_____

2 Apart from Sunday I don't think it rained at all last week.

_____

3 This shop has branches in Bath Bristol Cardiff and Penzance.

_____

4 Rudolph said "Why am I the only reindeer with a red nose?"

_____

Helpful Hint

Remember that **commas** can be used to separate items in a list, to make the meaning in a sentence clear and, like brackets, can be used to give extra information that is not part of the **main clause**.

(D) Write whether the underlined words are a noun phrase, a preposition phrase or a clause. [4]

Example: *Clear and blue, the swimming pool looked very inviting.* *noun phrase*

1 Carefully and falteringly, they walked to the mountain's summit.

_____

2 The sun, orange and harsh, glared down.

_____

3 The soldiers suddenly appeared over the hill.

_____

4 She closed the door before she went out.

_____

8

E) Turn these into simple sentences by removing all of the unnecessary words and detail. Just keep the words needed for each sentence to make sense. [5]

Example: *Before we begin to prepare any type of food, it is so important to wash our hands to ensure that good hygiene is followed.*

Before we prepare food, it is important to wash our hands.

> It can be very helpful to be able to identify the main information from extra description and detail in a piece of writing. Writing clearly and briefly, using simple sentences, means the information is easy to find.

1 Every time we go into town, we love to buy perfectly iced cupcakes and pretty little macaroons from the nearby bakery.

_____

2 Whenever I visit my friend Loren, which tends to be every Friday or Saturday, we spend most of the time talking.

_____

3 The two modern glass and steel blocks of flats stand proudly on the outskirts of town.

_____

4 Regardless of the long journey, we really must try to make time to see our older cousins this summer.

_____

5 Although it is often cold, we still like to paddle in the sea when we go on holiday to any of the coastal resorts.

_____

F) Underline the prepositions in these sentences. [5]

Example: *Tomas placed the lamp <u>on</u> the table <u>beside</u> the bed.*

1 The police moved among the crowd in the stadium.

2 The climbers on the ledge looked down at the injured woman.

3 Our village is near the farm shop and before the motorway.

4 They marched up the hill and rested beside the stream.

5 The tree stood near the house sheltering everything that grew underneath it.

10

Ⓖ Underline the determiner in each sentence then write whether it is an article, demonstrative, number, ordinal, possessive adjective or quantifier. [10]

Example: *Hand these tickets in at the counter.* demonstrative

1 Where are the scissors?

2 Can you help me find my keys?

3 Is there any post today?

4 There are eight boys playing outside.

5 Is there milk in the fridge?

6 Have you seen her pencil case?

7 I was looking for a plaster.

8 He found some clean tea towels and began drying up.

9 Hannah came in fourth place.

10 Have you seen this magazine article?

Ⓗ Underline the correct form of the verb to complete these sentences. [8]

Example: *We was/were on our way to the airport at last!*

1 Lily was/were driving Catherine to the station.

2 That goat will eat/ate almost anything!

3 The Year 5 children perform/performs in assembly.

4 I saw/seen the latest episode after I downloaded it.

5 The runners dressed as caterpillars finish/finished the race in record time.

6 Elsa was listening to the radio when she hear/heard the doorbell.

7 The sponge cake rise/rose beautifully in the oven.

8 I am/is learning to play the trumpet at school.

Helpful Hint

Always remember to make sure that the **verb** form agrees with the sentence subject.

18

Ⓐ Write out these sentences adding commas in the correct places. [5]

Example: *Bella our neighbour is training to be a vet.*

Bella, our neighbour, is training to be a vet.

1 The navy has different types of ship: destroyers frigates survey ships and mine hunters.

_____

2 Of all the museums the submarine museum is our favourite.

_____

3 You can do a guided tour explore as a group or wander at leisure.

_____

4 If you are not scared of small spaces go on board the 1901 midget submarine.

_____

5 "Well" said Jay "shall we go and have a look?"

_____

Ⓑ Fill in the gaps in the sentences using the past progressive form of the verb given in capitals. [6]

Example: *(STAND) The train was standing in the station.*

1 (SLEEP) Mum and Dad _____ in the deckchairs.

2 (READ) I _____ quietly in the library.

3 (SKETCH) We _____ in our drawing books.

4 (TEACH) Mr Kori _____ in the science labs.

5 (GNAW) The hamster _____ the piece of carrot.

6 (CATCH) We _____ the train to Crewe this time last week.

💡 **Helpful Hint**

Remember that the progressive form of the **verb** uses the words
'was' or 'were' and the 'ing' ending of the **verb**.

11

C Underline the verbs and circle the adverbs in these sentences. [6]

Example: *Zoe locked the door carefully behind her.*

1 The boys grumbled constantly all through the lesson.

2 We ate the cheese and pickle sandwiches greedily.

3 The little girl with pigtails tumbled awkwardly down the steps.

4 Impressively, Rachel and Marianne won the sandcastle competition.

5 Trevor and Rob studiously completed their homework.

6 Fortunately, I remembered my guitar.

D Use a line to join each fronted adverbial with the end of a sentence. [7]

1	Before we went to bed,	Nina rode her bike.
2	After the thunder,	Kai refilled the bird feeder.
3	Along the cycle path,	the plate smashed on the floor.
4	All morning,	Ana found her reading book.
5	Before I could catch it,	the lightning lit up the dark sky.
6	When it was empty,	we waited for the post to arrive.
7	Cleaning her room,	we brushed our teeth.

E Underline the main clauses in these compound sentences. [8]

Example: *The lid wasn't on properly so the sauce went everywhere!*

1 The rain fell continually or it certainly seemed that way.

2 Grey clouds had been gathering for days so we knew the rain was coming.

3 Abi was really tired because it had been a long day.

4 She'd had a great time with her friends as she hadn't seen them for ages.

5 Sammy hoped she could complete the marathon as she had trained so hard.

6 She had never taken on such a big challenge but her mum was sure she could do it.

7 There was a long queue at the post office so I went back later.

8 My auntie lives in India but she is coming to stay with us for a holiday.

21

Ⓕ Place a colon in the correct places in this text. [5]

Example: *Many birds can be seen in my garden robins, blackbirds and finches.*

Many birds can be seen in my garden: robins, blackbirds and finches.

1 It is important in a busy urban area to have green spaces they are a place for children to play and for people to meet each other.

2 If you are responsible for a park, it is important to
- make sure that plants are pruned so walkways are safe
- provide bins for litter and dog waste
- provide staff to monitor the park for signs of danger.

3 There are several poisonous plants hemlock, yew, foxgloves and laurel.

4 He recited from Wordsworth's famous poem "I wandered lonely as a cloud …"

5 You will need to bring two of the following forms of identification driving licence, passport, bank statement.

Ⓖ Add the words 'more' and 'most' to these adjectives to make comparative and superlative adjectives. [12]

Example: *beautiful* *more beautiful* *most beautiful*

1 important _____

2 colourful _____

3 expensive _____

4 crowded _____

5 careful _____

6 successful _____

7 honest _____

8 delicious _____

9 amazing _____

10 brutal _____

11 traditional _____

12 horrible _____

The letters 'er' and 'est' are usually used to make **comparative** and **superlative adjectives**. However, if the root word has two or more syllables, the words 'more' (for the **comparative**) and 'most' (for the **superlative**) are used before the **adjective**.

Example: bashful, more bashful, most bashful.

17

(H) Add apostrophes in the right places to show single or plural possession. [10]

Example: *Mr Shaw has a car and the boys have bikes.* Mr Shaw's car and the boys' bikes.

1   Mrs Rand has toast and Mr Rand has some cereal.

_____

2   Those shops have bargains and this shop has the best prices.

_____

3   Our family has tents and those families have caravans.

_____

4   Tinkerbell has a magic wand and Peter has a tuneful pipe.

_____

5   The cats have new toys and the dog has a new bed.

_____

6   The villages have playing fields and the town has a swimming pool.

_____

7   The planes have wings and the helicopters have rotor blades.

_____

8   The phone has a camera and the computer has a printer.

_____

9   The book has chapters and the chapters have paragraphs.

_____

10 The artist has brushes and the writers have pens.

_____

10

Ⓐ Write out these sentences adding commas in the correct places. [5]

Example: *The shop sells cards wrapping paper envelopes and gift tags.*

The shop sells cards, wrapping paper, envelopes and gift tags.

1   A person who studies flies as opposed to all insects is a dipterist.

_____

2   No I did not know that the French word for fly is 'mouche'.

_____

3   The teacher said "There are more than 7000 types of fly in the UK."

_____

4   Although they only live for a month a housefly goes through four life stages.

_____

5   Many different flies are found in the UK: lacewings bluebottles horseflies and houseflies.

_____

Ⓑ Fill in the gaps in the sentences using the past progressive form of the verb given in capitals. [6]

Example: *(STOP) The police officer was stopping the traffic.*

1   (RUN) We _____ around the playground.

2   (KNIT) Grandpa _____ a scarf for grandma for her birthday.

3   (HOPE) I _____ you would help me with this project.

4   (TALK) They _____ loudly in the conservatory.

5   (RIP) We _____ up the old cardboard box when the phone rang.

6   (GO) I _____ into the garden to peg out the washing.

💡 **Helpful Hint**

Remember to use 'was' or 'were' and add the 'ing' ending of the **verb**. You may need to make a change to the spelling of the **verb** to add the 'ing'.

11

Ⓒ Underline the determiner in each sentence then write whether it is an article, demonstrative, number, ordinal, possessive adjective or quantifier. [6]

Example: *Can we use <u>your</u> football?* *possessive adjective*

1   Where can I get the best deal?   _____

2   Where is my hairbrush?   _____

3   Is there much washing up to do?   _____

4   It is my birthday tomorrow!   _____

5   Have you got any natural yoghurt?   _____

6   It rained every day on holiday.   _____

Ⓓ Underline the verbs and circle the adverbs in these sentences. [6]

Example: *The choir <u>sang</u> (tunefully) in the concert.*

1   Sophie was happily playing with her sister, Molly.

2   The prime minister spoke earnestly to the crowd of reporters.

3   The camels strode steadily between the sand dunes.

4   Mrs Campbell successfully taught in this school for many years.

5   The leaves fluttered gently in the summer breeze.

6   The decorator skilfully painted the grand ballroom.

Ⓔ Underline the main clauses in these compound sentences. [6]

Example: *<u>It was nearly the end of term</u> and <u>we couldn't wait for the holidays!</u>*

1   It is the big football match today so the town centre will be busy.

2   We had our hair cut but our usual hairdresser was not there.

3   You could have some fruit or you may prefer to have yoghurt instead.

4   I have never been to Canada but I would love to go there.

5   The Highlands of Scotland are amazing but they can be dangerous in the winter months.

6   I am going to Charlotte's party and my cousin is also invited.

18

F Write out these sentences placing a semi-colon between the two clauses. [5]

Example: *Beth ran to the top of the hill she paused to catch her breath.*

Beth ran to the top of the hill; she paused to catch her breath.

1 We had a collection of buckets and spades we took building sandcastles seriously.

_____

2 Jessie had a new football game she couldn't wait to try it.

_____

3 The boys were very noisy they were disturbing everyone.

_____

4 Tavleen was excited she had new shoes to wear for the celebrations.

_____

5 Jasper loved painting he mixed blue and red to make deep purple.

_____

G Turn the negative sentences into positive sentences by removing the words 'never', 'not' or 'no'. [4]

Example: *Mei never has enough time for breakfast.*

Mei has enough time for breakfast.

1 Phoebe never visited her aunt in Norwich.

_____

2 Stacey did not have time to rest before the next race.

_____

3 Logan never saw his friends at the swimming pool.

_____

4 Kit and Seb did not get on the train.

_____

9

(H) Turn these into simple sentences by removing all of the unnecessary words and detail. Just keep the words needed for each sentence to make sense. [8]

Example: *The many constellations of stars shone and twinkled brightly in the clear night sky.*

The stars shone in the night sky.

1   The sparkling diamond ring was irresistible for the light-fingered thief so he quickly stole it and put it away in his coat pocket.

_____

2   Footballers have a really demanding fitness regime to keep them at their peak so they are always able to perform at their very best.

_____

3   We all had amazing fun when we went hover-boarding on our active and adventurous holiday!

_____

4   Scientists are now researching how to repair our nerves, which will really give a lot of help to people who have to live with pain or nerve damage.

_____

5   Paul walked across the green and grassy hills and saw lots of wildlife in the beautiful county of Yorkshire.

_____

6   As the curtains rose, I felt extremely nervous when I realised at that moment that I was on stage in front of such an unexpectedly large audience.

_____

7   As night fell, the orange and yellow firelight flickered brightly in the darkness of the room.

_____

8   Energetic and rhythmic music was playing loudly from the speakers on the radio.

_____

8

Test your skills

Change these adjectives to make comparative and superlative adjectives.

1 sunny _____

2 adaptable _____

3 brave _____

Turn these sentences into the past tense.

4 (BUY) We _____ our tickets for the cinema.

5 (KNOW) I _____ all the words for the spelling test.

6 (POUR) The water _____ in through the crack in the ceiling.

Underline the prepositions in these sentences.

7 The palace was built in a beautiful setting by the river.

8 My brother was sitting near the window and beside the fireplace.

Underline the determiner in each sentence then write whether it is an article, demonstrative, number, ordinal, possessive adjective or quantifier.

9 Who was first to arrive? _____

10 I would like to order a sandwich, please. _____

11 Where is that book? _____

12 We need to bake five cakes. _____

Underline the main clauses in these compound sentences.

13 Daffodils are spring bulbs whereas dahlias are summer bulbs.

14 Mixing blue and yellow makes green but varying the amount of each colour changes the shade.

15 Hockey is played with a stick but tennis is played with a racquet.

Underline the fronted adverbials in these sentences.

16 Although the scenery was fantastic, it was too hot to sit out.

17 Whenever we go camping, we always take a good torch.

18 However, you must make the safety of yourself and others the first priority.

19 As long as you are home by teatime, you can go out with your friends this afternoon.

19

Write out these sentences placing a semi-colon between the two clauses.

20 Haru and Tom visited Alex he had been ill with the flu.

_____

21 The wood panelling was gorgeous it was typical of a Tudor building.

_____

Change these third-person sentences into the first person.

22 Lily-Ann was off to her gymnastics class.

_____

23 Ruby and Dewi were playing with Alima in her garden.

_____

24 She stubbed her toe against the table leg.

_____

Underline the verbs and circle the adverbs in these sentences.

25 The huge creature steadily swam towards the shore.

26 Dev generously shared his crayons with the girls.

27 The warehouse was packed solidly with crates.

28 He smiled broadly at the waiting crowd.

Write one word in the space to make the correct form of the verb given in capitals.

29 (BAKE) She _____ a cake for the party when the telephone rang.

30 (GO) I _____ to visit the doctor last week.

31 (BREAK) I was so clumsy that I _____ my glasses.

Write whether the underlined words are a noun phrase, a preposition phrase or a clause.

32 The <u>thorny brambles and weeds</u> were taking over the garden. _____

33 <u>Halfway between</u> the villages stood the farmer's old barn. _____

14

Turn the positive sentences into negative sentences by adding or replacing words with 'never', 'none' or 'nothing'.

34 My bedroom is almost neat and tidy!

_____

35 There is something you can do to get ready for the holiday.

_____

Put an apostrophe in the right place to show single or plural possession.

36 This book has a torn cover. _____

37 Those jars have labels. _____

38 These elephants have trunks. _____

Turn these into simple sentences by removing all of the unnecessary words and detail. Just keep the words needed for each sentence to make sense.

39 The prettily meandering brook babbled over stones and pebbles as it flowed from its source on the top of the hill into the river.

_____

40 The irritating beeping sound of Rupa's much-hated alarm clock broke through her dream and woke her.

_____

Write out these sentences adding commas in the correct places.

41 The hand-knitted blanket was in shades of pink cream purple and blue.

_____

42 Rosie said "Yes I enjoy crafts but it is hard to find time for them all!"

_____

43 The little babies all lying in their cots slept contentedly.

_____

44 "I know" said Mrs David sympathetically. "It can be really tricky" she continued.

_____

11

Place a colon in the correct place in each sentence.

45 Miss Dembenski's poster has a great message "Always do your best and that is enough."

46 There are four things you need a pencil, ruler, pen and eraser.

47 Sherry is a lovely horse she has such a gentle manner.

48 You should
- write your name on each page
- read each question carefully
- answer every question
- check your answers before you hand in your paper.

Put an apostrophe in the correct place to show possession.

49 Marly has a book. _____

50 The flock has a shepherd. _____

51 Our bicycles have wheels. _____

7

Key words

abstract noun abstract nouns are ideas or feelings and cannot be touched, seen or heard, for example *anger, beauty*

adjective a word that describes a noun

adverb a word that describes a verb

article a type of determiner, for example *a, an*

clause a simple sentence that can be joined to another clause by using a conjunction

collective noun collective nouns refer to groups of people or things

colon (:) two dots used to introduce lists, examples or explanations

comma (,) a punctuation mark used to separate items in a list

common noun the name of an object, for example *book, apple*

comparative adjective a word used to compare two things, for example *faster*

compound sentence a sentence with two main clauses linked by a joining word

conjunction a word that joins two clauses together

demonstrative a type of determiner, for example *that, those*

determiner a word that comes before a noun in order to give more information about it

direct speech when someone's exact words are quoted, for example *"I love puppies"*

first person from the writer's point of view, for example *I am going to the shop*

fronted adverbial a phrase containing an adverb that is placed in front of the main part of a sentence

inverted commas (" ") also known as speech marks, these are used to show direct speech

main clause a clause that makes sense on its own

narrative a story or account of events

noun phrase a group of words that has a noun as its key word

ordinal a type of determiner that show the order of events, for example *First add sugar, next add milk*

phrase a group of words that can be understood as a unit

plural a noun becomes plural when it describes more than one thing

plural possession when something has more than one owner, for example *my parents' house*

possession when something has one owner, for example *my mum's house*

preposition a word that describes the location of the noun

preposition phrase part of a sentence that begins with a preposition, followed by a noun, pronoun or noun phrase

present perfect tense describing something that happened and is still relevant now or is still happening now

present tense describing what is happening now

proper noun names of people and places, days of the week, months of the year, titles and organisations

quantifier a type of determiner that shows us how many, for example *I have two dogs*

second person when the writer appears to be speaking to or about the reader, for example *You can find the answers in the middle of this book*

semi-colon (;) a punctuation mark used to separate two sentences or main clauses of equal importance

simple past tense describing something that happened in the past

singular a noun describing to one thing

subordinate clause part of a sentence that adds meaning to the main clause but cannot be used as a sentence on its own

superlative adjective a word used to compare more than two things, for example *fastest*

third person when the writer is describing someone else's point of view, for example *He thought it was beautiful*

verb a word that identifies an action

Progress chart

How did you do? Fill in your score below and shade in the corresponding boxes to compare your progress across the different tests and units.

50%   100%   50%   100

Unit 1, p3 Score: __ / 18

Unit 6, p27 Score: __ / 11

Unit 1, p4 Score: __ / 14

Unit 6, p28 Score: __ / 7

Unit 1, p5 Score: __ / 18

Unit 6, p29 Score: __ / 17

Unit 1, p6 Score: __ / 10

Quick quiz, p30 Score: __ / 16

Unit 2, p7 Score: __ / 16

Unit 7, p31 Score: __ / 17

Unit 2, p8 Score: __ / 13

Unit 7, p32 Score: __ / 8

Unit 2, p9 Score: __ / 11

Unit 7, p33 Score: __ / 10

Unit 2, p10 Score: __ / 14

Unit 7, p34 Score: __ / 18

Unit 3, p11 Score: __ / 10

Unit 8, p35 Score: __ / 11

Unit 3, p12 Score: __ / 16

Unit 8, p36 Score: __ / 21

Unit 3, p13 Score: __ / 11

Unit 8, p37 Score: __ / 17

Quick quiz, p14 Score: __ / 17

Unit 8, p38 Score: __ / 10

Unit 4, p15 Score: __ / 16

Unit 9, p39 Score: __ / 11

Unit 4, p16 Score: __ / 12

Unit 9, p40 Score: __ / 18

Unit 4, p17 Score: __ / 15

Unit 9, p41 Score: __ / 9

Unit 4, p18 Score: __ / 12

Unit 9, p42 Score: __ / 8

Unit 5, p19 Score: __ / 18

Unit 10, p43 Score: __ / 19

Unit 5, p20 Score: __ / 14

Unit 10, p44 Score: __ / 14

Unit 5, p21 Score: __ / 14

Unit 10, p45 Score: __ / 11

Unit 5, p22 Score: __ / 14

Unit 10, p46 Score: __ / 7